On the Harmony
of Religions and
Philosophy

Ibn Rushd

Translated by Mohammed Jamil-al-Rahman

DODO PRESS

On the Harmony of Religions and Philosophy
by Ibn Rushd, translated by Mohammed Jamil-al-Rahman

1921

Contents

The Creation of the Universe

The Law teaches that the universe was invented and created by God, and that it did not come into being by chance or by itself. The method adopted by the Law for proving this is not the one upon which the Asharites have depended. For we have already shown that those methods are not specially certain for the learned, nor common enough to satisfy all the classes of men. The methods which are really serviceable are those which have a very few premises, and the results of which fall very near to the commonly known ideas. But in instructing the common people the Law does not favor statements composed of long and complete reasoning, based upon different problems. So everyone who, in teaching them, adopts a different course, and interprets the Law according to it, has lost sight of its purpose and gone astray from the true path. And so also, the Law in giving illustrations for its reasoning uses only those which are present before us.

Whatever has been thought necessary for the common people to know, has been explained to them by the nearest available examples, as in the case of the day of Judgment. But whatever was unnecessary for them to know, they have been told that it was beyond their knowledge, as the words of God about the Soul [Qur'an 22.85]. Now that we have established this, it is necessary that the method adopted by the Law for teaching the creation of the universe to the common people be such as would be acknowledged by all. It is also necessary that since there cannot be found anything present to illustrate the creation of the universe the Law must have used the examples of the creation of things in the visible world.

So the method adopted by Law is that the universe was made by God. If we look intently into the verse pertaining to this subject we shall see that the method adopted is that of divine solicitude, which we know to be one of those which prove the existence of God. When a man sees a thing made in a certain shape, proportion and fashion, for a particular advantage is derived from it, and purpose which is to be attained, so that it becomes clear to him, that had it not been found in that shape, and proportion, then that advantage would have been wanting in it, he comes to know for certain that there is a maker of that thing, and that he had made it in that shape and proportion, for a set purpose. For it is not possible that all those qualities serving that purpose be collected in that thing by chance alone. For instance, if a man sees a stone on the ground in a shape fit for sitting, and finds its proportions and fashion of the same kind, then he would come to know that it was made by a maker, and that he had made it and placed it there. But when he sees nothing in it which may have made it fit for sitting then he becomes certain that its existence in the place was by chance only, without its being fashioned by any maker.

Such is also the case with the whole of the universe. For when a man sees the sun, the moon, and all the stars, which are the cause of the four seasons; of days and nights, of rain, water and winds, of the inhabitation of the parts of the earth, of the existence of man, and of the being of all the animals and the plants and of the earth being fit for the habitation of a man, and other animals living in it; and the water fit for the animals living in it; and the air fit for birds, and if there be anything amiss in this creation and edifice, the whole world would come to confusion and disorder, then he would come to know with certainty that it is not possible that this harmony in it for the different members of the universe — man, animals, and plants — be found by chance only.

He will know that there is one who determined it, and so one who made it by intention, and that is God, exalted and magnified may He be. He would know with certainty that the universe is a created thing, for he would necessarily think that it is not possible that in it should be found all this harmony, if it be not made by someone, and had come into existence by chance alone. This kind of argument, is quite definite and at the same time clear, and some have mentioned it here. It is based upon two principles which are acknowledged by all. One of them being, that the universe, with all its component parts, is found fit for the existence of man and things; secondly, that which is found suitable in all its parts, for a single purpose, leading to a single goal, is necessarily a created thing. So those two principles lead us naturally to admit that the universe is a created thing, and that there is a maker of it. Hence "the argument of analogy" leads to two things at one and the same time, and that is why it is the best argument for proving the existence of God. This kind of reasoning is also found in the Qur'an in many verses in which the creation of the universe is mentioned.

For instance, "Have We not made the earth a bed, and the mountains for shelter to fix the same? And have We not created you of two sexes; and appointed your sleep for rest and made the night a garment to cover you, and destined the day to a gaining of a livelihood; and built over you seven heavens, and placed therein a burning lamp? And do We not send down from the clouds pressing forth rain, water pouring down in abundance, that We may hereby produce corn and herbs, and gardens planted thick with trees" [Qur'an 77.3ff]. If we ponder over this verse it would be found that our attention has been called to the suitability of the different parts of the universe for the existence of man. In the very beginning we are informed of a fact well-known to all — and that is that the earth has been created in a way which has made it suitable for our existence. Had it been unstable, or of any other shape, or in any other place, or not of the present proportion, it would not have been possible to be here, or at all created on it. All this is included in the words, "Have We not made the earth a bed for you"? for in a bed are collected together all the qualities of shape, tranquility, and peace, to which may be added those of smoothness and softness.

So how strange is this wonderful work and how excellent this blessedness, and how wonderful this collection of all the qualities! This is so because in the word mihad (bed) are brought together all those qualities, which are found in the earth, rendering it suitable for the existence of man. It is a thing which becomes clear to the learned after much learning and a long time, "But God will appropriate His mercy unto whom He pleases [Qur'an 2.99]. Then as to the divine words, "And the mountains for stakes," — they tell us of the advantage to be found in the tranquility of the earth on account of the mountains. For had the earth been created smaller than it is now, that is, without mountains, it would have been quivered by the motion of other elements, the water and the air, and would have been shaken and thus displaced. This would naturally have been the cause of the destruction of the animal world. So when its tranquility is in harmony with those living on it, it did not come into being by chance alone, but was made by someone's intention, and determination. Certainly it was made by One who intended it, and determined it, for the sake of those living on it.

Then He calls our attention to the suitability of the existence of night and day for animals. He says "And made the night a garment to cover you; and destined the day to a gaining of your livelihood. " He means to say that He has made the night like a covering and clothing for all the things, from the heat of the sun. For had there been no setting of the sun at night, all the things, whose life has been made dependent upon the sun, would have perished — that is, the animals and the plants. As clothing protects the people from the heat of the sun, in addition to its being a covering, so God likened the night to it. This is one of the most beautiful of the metaphors. There is also another advantage in the night for the animals: their sleep in it is very deep, after the setting of the sun, which keeps faculties in motion, that is, wide awake. So God has said, "And appointed your sleep for rest, " on account of the darkness of the night. Then He says, "And built over you seven heavens, and placed therein a burning lamp." Here by the word building He means their creation, and their harmony with the created things, and their arrangement and system. By strength He means that power of revolution and motion which is never slackened, and never overtaken by fatigue; and they never fall like other roofs and high edifices. To this refer the words of God, "And made the heaven a roof well-supported" [Qur'an 21.33]. By all this He shows their fitness in number, shape, fashion, and movement, for the existence of those who live on the earth round it. Were one of the heavenly bodies, not to speak of all, to stop for a moment all would be chaos on the face of the earth. Some people think the blast of the last trumpet, which will be the cause of the thunderbolt, will be nothing but a stop in the revolution of the heavenly bodies.

Then He tells us of the advantage of the sun for those living on the earth and says, "And placed therein a burning lamp. " He calls it a lamp because in reality it is all darkness, and light covers the darkness of the night, and if there be no lamp, man can get no advantage out of his sense of sight at nighttime; and in the same way if there were no sun the animals can have no benefit of their sense of seeing. He calls our attention to this advantage of the suns ignoring others because it is the noblest of all the advantages and the most-apparent of all. Then He tells us of His kindness in sending down rain, for the sake of the plants and the animals. The coming down of rain in an appointed proportion, and at an appointed season, for the cultivated fields cannot be by chance alone, but is the result of divine solicitude for us all. So He says, "And do We not send down from the clouds pressing forth rain, water pouring down in abundance that We may hereby produce corn and herbs, and gardens planted thick with trees."

There are many verses of the Qur'an on this subject. For instance, He says, "Do you not see how God has created the seven heavens, one above another, and has placed the moon therein for a light, and has appointed the sun for a taper? God has also provided and caused you to bring forth wheat from the earth" [Qur'an 71.14-16]. If we were to count all such verses and comment upon them showing the kindness of the Creator for the created, it would take too many volumes. We do not intend to do it in this book. If God should grant us life and leisure we shall write a book to show the kindness of God to which He has called our attention.

It should be known that this kind of argument is just contrary to that which the Asharites think leads to the knowledge of God. They think that the creation does not lead us to the knowledge of God through any of His goodness, but through possibility, that is, the possibility which is found in all things, which we can understand to be of his shape or of quite a contrary one. But if this possibility be found alike in both the cases, then there is no wisdom in the creation of the universe, and there is found no harmony between man and the parts of it. For, as they think, if it is possible for the things to have any other form than they have now, then there can exist no harmony between man and other existent things by the creation of which God has obliged man and commanded him to be thankful to Him. This opinion, by which the creation of man, as a part of the universe, is just as possible, for instance, as his creation in the void, is like the opinion of those who say that man exists but he could have been created in quite a different shape, and yet could perform actions like a man. According to them it is also possible that he may have formed the part of another universe quite different from the existing one. In that case the blessing of the universe can have no obligation for man, for they are not necessary for his purpose. Hence man is quite careless of them and they of him. So their existence is no blessing to him. This is all against the nature of man.

On the whole, a man who denies the existence of the effects arranged according to the causes in the question of arts, or whose wisdom cannot understand it, then he has no knowledge of the art of its Maker. So also a man who denies the existence of an order of effects in accordance with causes in this universe, denies the existence of the Creator altogether. Their saying that God is above these causes, and that they cannot have any bearing on the effects by His command, is very far from the true nature of philosophy, nay, it is a destroyer of it. For if it is possible to have the same effects with other than the prescribed causes just in the same degree as by them, then where is the greatness in producing the effects from the known Causes? It is so because the effects from the causes have one of the following three reasons. Either the existence of the causes will be in place of the effects by compulsion, as a man's taking his food; or their being more perfect, that is, the effect becoming better and more perfect through them, as a man's having two eyes, or they may have neither a better nor a more compulsive effect. In this case the existence of the effect and the cause would be by chance, without any intention at all; and, hence, there would be no greatness found in it.

For instance, if the shape of a human hand, the number of the fingers, and their length be neither necessary nor adding any perfection in its work in seizing things of different kind, then the actions of the hand from this shape, and number of parts, would be by chance alone. If it be so, then it makes no difference whether a man is given a hand or a hoof, or something else, like the different animals, for their particular actions. On the whole, if we ignore the causes and their effects, then there remains nothing to refute the arguments of those who believe in the creation of the universe by chance alone, that is, those who say that there is no Creator at all, and that which has come into being in this universe is the result of material causes. For taking one of the two alternatives it is not more possible that it may have happened by chance, than done by an independent Actor. So when the Asharites say that the existence of one or more possibilities shows that there is a particular Maker of these things, they can answer and say that the existence of things by one of these possibilities was by chance alone, for intention works as one of the causes, and that which happens without any means or cause is by chance. We see that many things come into being in this way. For example, the elements mix together by chance, and then by this unintentional mixing there is produced a new thing. They mix again, and this quite unintentionally produces quite a new thing. In this way every kind of creation may be said to have come into existence by chance.

We say that it is necessary that there be found order and arrangement, the more perfect and finished than what can be imagined. This mixing together of elements is limited and prearranged, and things produced by them are sure to happen, and no disorder has ever happened in them. But all this could not happen by chance alone, for that which happens in this way by chance is of the least value. It is to this that God refers, "It is the work of the Lord, who has rightly disposed all things" [Qur'an 27.90]. I would like to know what completeness can be found in things made by chance, for such things are by no means better than their opposites. To this God refers in the following words, "You cannot see in the Creation of the most Merciful any unfitness or disproportion. Lift your eyes again to heaven, and look whether you see any flaw" [Qur'an 67.3]. But what defect can be greater than that all the things can be found with any other quality than they really possess. For the non-existent quality may be better than the existing one. In this way, if one thinks that were the Eastern movement to become Western and vice-versa, there would be no difference in the universe then he has destroyed philosophy altogether. He is like a man who thinks that were the right side of the animals to become left, and vice-versa, there would be no difference at all, for one of the two alternatives is there. For as it is possible to say that it is made according to one alternative by an independent Maker, so it is possible to assert that it was all made by chance alone. For we see so many things coming into being by themselves.

It is quite clear to you that all the people see that lower kinds of creation could have been made in a different way from that in which they really are, and as they see this lower degree in many things they think that they must have been made by chance. But in the higher creation they know that it is impossible to have been made in a more perfect and excellent form than that given to it by the Creator. So this opinion, which is one of the opinions of the Mutakallimun is both against the Law and philosophy. What we say is that the opinion of possibility in creation is closer to a complete denial of God, than leading us nearer to Him. At the same time it falsifies philosophy. For if we do not understand that there is a mean between the beginnings and ends of the Creation, upon which is based the ends of things, then there can neither be any order nor any method in it. And if they be wanting then there can be no proof of the existence of an intelligent and knowing Maker; for taking them together with cause and effect we are led to the fact that they must have been created by wisdom and knowledge.

But, on the other hand, the existence of either of two possibilities shows that they may have been performed by a not-knowing Maker and by chance alone. Just as a stone falling on the earth may fall in any place, on any side, and in any form. It will show the want of the existence either of a creator at all or at least of a wise and knowing Creator. The thing which has compelled the Mutakallimun of the Asharites to adopt this opinion is a denial of the action of those natural forces which God has put in all things, as He has endowed them with life, power and so forth. They avoided the opinion that there was any other creator but God, and God forbid that there be any other, for he is the only creator of the causes and they are made effective by His command only. We will talk of this in detail when discoursing on Fate and Predestination. They were also afraid that by admitting the natural causes they might be accused of saying that the universe came into being by chance only. They would have known that a denial of it means a denial of a great part of the arguments, which can be advanced for a proof of the existence of God. One who denies any part of God's creation denies His work, which falls very near to a denial of a part of His attributes.

On the whole as their opinion is based upon hasty conclusions, which come to the mind of a man by superficial thought and as apparently it appears that the word "intention" can be applied to one who has power to do bad or otherwise, they saw that if they did not admit that all the creation is possible, they would not be able to say that it came into existence by the action of an intending creator. So they say that all the creation is possible so that they may prove that the creator is an intelligent one. They never thought of the order which is necessary in things made, and with that their coming from an intelligent creator. These people have also ignored the blame they will have to bear in thus denying wisdom to the creator; or maintaining that chance should be found governing creation. They know, as we have said, that it is necessary, on account of the order existent in nature, that it must have been brought into being by some knowing creator, otherwise the order found in it would be by chance. When they were compelled to deny the natural forces they had to deny with them a large number of those forces which God has made subservient to His command for the creation and preservation of things. For God has created some things from causes which He has produced from outside, these are the heavenly bodies; there are other things which He has made by causes placed in the things themselves, that is; the soul, and other natural forces, by which he preserves those things. So how wicked is the man who destroys philosophy, and "invented a lie about God" [Qur'an 3.88].

This is only a part of the change which has taken place in the Law, in this and other respects, which we have already mentioned, and will mention hereafter. From all this it must have become clear to you that the method which God had adopted for teaching His creatures that the universe is made and created by Him is the method of kindness and wisdom, towards all His creatures and especially towards man. It is a method which bears the same relation to our intellect, as the sun bears to our senses. The method which it has adopted towards the common people about this problem is that of illustration from things observed. But as there was nothing which could be given as an illustration, and as the common people cannot understand a thing, an illustration of which they cannot see, God tells us that the universe was created in a certain time out of a certain thing, which He made. He tells us his condition before the creation of the universe, "His throne was above the waters" [Qur'an 11.9]. He also says, "Verily your Lord is God who created the heavens and the earth in six days" [Qur'an 7.52], and "Then He set His mind to the creation of the heavens, and it was smoke" [Qur'an 12.10]. In addition to these there are other verses of the Book, pertaining to this subject. So it is incumbent that nothing out of them should be interpreted for the common people, and nothing should be presented to them in explaining it but this illustration. For one who changes it, makes the wisdom of the Law useless. If it be said that the Law teaches about the universe that it is created, and made out of nothing and in no time, then it is a thing which even the learned cannot understand, not to speak of the common people. So we should not deviate in this matter of the Law.

The Advent of the Prophets

If we admit the existence of the prophetic mission, by putting the idea of possibility, which is in fact ignorance, in place of certainty, and make miracles a proof of the truth of man who claims to be a prophet it becomes necessary that they should not be used by a person, who says that they can be performed by others than prophets, as the Mutakallimun do. They think that the miracles can be performed by the magicians and saints. The condition which they attach with them is that miracles prove a man to be a prophet, when he at the same time claims to be so, for the true prophet can perform them as opposed to the false ones. This is an argument without any proof, for it can be understood either by hearing or reason That is, it is said that one whose claims to prophecy are wrong, cannot perform miracles, but as we have already said, when they cannot be performed by a liar, then they can only be done by the good people, whom God has meant for this purpose. These people, if they speak a lie, are not good, and hence cannot perform the miracles. But this does not satisfy the people who think miracles to be possible from the magicians, for they certainly are not good men. It is here that the weakness of the argument lies. Hence some people have thought that the best thing is to believe that they cannot be performed but by the prophets.

It is clear to you from the life of the prophet, peace be upon him, that he never invited any man or community

15

to believe in his prophecy, and that which he has brought with him from God, by means of the performance of any miracles in support of his claim, such as changing one element into another. Whatever miracles did appear from him were only performed in the natural course of things, without on his part any intention of contention or competition. The following words of the Qur'an will make this clear "And they say: We will by no means believe in you, until you cause a spring of water to gush forth for us out of the earth, and you have a garden of palm-trees and vines, and you cause rivers to spring forth from the midst thereof in abundance; or you cause the heaven to fall down in pieces upon us, as you have given out, or you bring down God and the angels to vouch for you; or you have a house of gold, or you ascend by a ladder to heaven; neither will we believe your ascending there alone, until you cause a book to descend unto us, bearing witness of you which we may read. Answer: My Lord be praised, Am I other than a man sent as an apostle?" [Qur'an 17.92-95]. Then again, "Nothing hindered us from sending you with miracles, except that the former nations have charged them with imposture" [Qur'an 17.61].

The thing by which we invited the people to believe in him, and with which he vied with them is the Qur'an. For, says God, "Say, verily, if men and jinn were purposely assembled, that they might produce a book like this Qur'an, they could not produce one like unto it, although the one of them assigned the other" [Qur'an 17.90]. Then further, he says, "will they say, He hath forged the Qur'an? Answer, bring therefore ten chapters like unto it forged by yourself" [Qur'an 11.16]. This being the case the miracle of the Prophet with which he vied with the people and which he advanced as an argument for the truth of his claim to the prophetic mission, was the Qur'an. If it be said that this is quite clear, but how does it appear that the Qur'an is a mirage, and that it proves his prophecy, while just now we have proved the weakness of the proof of prophecy by means of miracles without any exceptions in the case of any prophet. Besides, the people have differed in taking the Qur'an to be a miracle at all. For in their opinion one of the conditions of a miracle is that it should be quite different from any act which may have become habitual. But the Qur'an is of this sort, because it is only words, though it excels all created words. So it becomes a miracle by its superiority only, that is, the impossibility for people bringing anything like it, on account of its being highly eloquent. This being the case, it differs from the habitual, not in genus but in details only, and that which differs in this way is of the same genus.

Some people say that it is a miracle by itself, and not by its superiority. They do not lay it down as a condition for miracles that they should be quite different from the habitual, but think that it should be such a habitual act, as men may fall short of accomplishing. We would reply that it is as the objectors say, but the thing about it is not as they have thought. That the Qur'an is an evidence of his prophecy, is based, we believe, upon two principles, which are found in the Book itself. The first being that the existence of the class of men called prophets and apostles is well-known. They are the men who lay down laws for

17

the people by divine revelation, and not by human education. Their existence can be denied only by the people who deny repeated action, as the existence of all things which we have not seen — the lives of the famous thinkers and so forth. All the philosophers, and other men are agreed, except those who pay no regard to their words, (and they are the Materialists), that there are men to whom have been revealed many commandments for the people, to perform certain good actions, by which their beatitude may be perfected; and to make them give up certain wrong beliefs and vicious actions. This is the business of divine apostles.

The second principle is, that everyone who does this work, that is, lays down laws by revelation, is a prophet. This principle is also quite in accordance with human nature. For as it is known that the business of medicine is to cure a disease, and one who can cure is a physician, so it is also known that the business of the prophets is to give law to the people by divine revelation, and one who does so is a prophet. The Book mentions the first principle in the following: "Verily We have revealed Our will unto you, as We have revealed it unto Noah, and the prophets who succeeded him, and We have revealed it unto Abraham, and Ishmael, and Isaac and Jacob, and the tribes, and unto Jesus, and Job, and Jonas, and Aaron and Solomon; and we have given you the Qur'an as We gave the Psalms unto David; some apostles have We sent, whom We have mentioned unto you, and God spoke unto Moses discoursing with him" [Qur'an 4.161-162], and again: "Say, I am not alone among the apostles" [Qur'an 46.8].

The second principle is that Mohammed, peace be upon him, has done the work of a prophet, that is, has given Law to the people by divine revelation. This also can be known from the Qur'an, where God mentions it. He says, "O men, now is an evident proof come unto you from your Lord, and We have sent down unto you manifest light" [Qur'an 4.173]. By manifest light is meant the Qur'an. Again He says, "O men, now is the apostle come unto you from your Lord; believe, therefore, it will be better for you" [Qur'an 4.168], and again, "But those among them who are well-grounded in knowledge, and faithful, who believe in that which has been sent down unto you, and that which has been sent down unto the prophets before you" [Qur'an 4.160]; and again "God is the witness of the revelation which He has sent down unto you; He sent it down with his special knowledge; the angels are also witness thereof; but God is a sufficient witness" [Qur'an 4.164].

Of Fate And Predestination

This is one of the most intricate problems of religion. For if you look into the traditional arguments (Hadith) about this problem you will find them contradictory; such also being the case with arguments of reason. The contradiction in the arguments of the first kind is found in the Qur'an and the Hadith. There are many verses of the Qur'an, which by their universal nature teach that all the things are predestined and that man is compelled to do his acts; then there are verses which say that man is free in his acts and not compelled in performing them. The following verses tell us that all the things are by compulsion, and are predestined, "Everything have We created bound by a fixed degree" [Qur'an 56.49]; again, "With Him everything is regulated according to a determined measure" [Qur'an 13.9]. Further, He says, "No accident happened in the earth, nor in your persons, but the same was entered in the Book verily it is easy with God" [Qur'an 57.22]. There may be quoted many other verses on this subject.

Now, as to the verses which say that man can acquire deeds by free will, and that things are only possible and not necessary, the following may be quoted: "Or He destroys them (by ship-wreck), because of that which their crew have merited; though He pardons many things" [Qur'an 42.32]. And again, "Whatever misfortune befalls you is sent you by God, for that which your hands have deserved" [Qur'an 42.32]. Further, He says, "But they who commit evil, equal thereunto" [Qur'an 10.28]. Again, He says, "It shall have the good which it gains, and it shall have the evil which it gains" [Qur'an 2.278]. And, "And as to Thamud, We directed them, but they loved blindness better than the true directions" [Qur'an 41.16].

Sometimes contradiction appears even in a single verse of the Qur'an. For instance, He says, "After a misfortune has befallen you (you had already attained two equal advantages), do you say, whence comes this? Answer, This is from yourselves" [Qur'an 3.159]. In the next verse, He says, "And what happened unto you, on the day whereon the two armies met, was certainly by permission of the Lord" [Qur'an 3.160]. Of this kind also is the verse, "Whatever good befalls you, O man, it is from God; and whatever evil befalls you, it is from yourself" [Qur'an 4.81]; while the preceding verse says, "All is from God" [Qur'an 4.80].

Such is also the case with the hadith. The Prophet says, "Every child is born in the true religion; his parents afterwards turn him into a Jew or a Christian." On another occasion he said, "The following people have been created for hell, and do the deeds of those who are fit for it. These have been created for heaven, and do deeds fit for it." The first hadith says that the cause of disbelief is one's own environments; while faith and belief are natural to man. The other hadith says that wickedness and disbelief are created by God, and man is compelled to follow them.

This condition of things has led Muslims to be divided into two groups. The one believed that man's wickedness or virtue is his own acquirement, and that according to these he will be either punished or rewarded. These are the Mutazilites. The belief of the other party is quite opposed to this. They say that man is compelled to do his deeds. They are the Jabarites. The Asharites have tried to adopt a mean between these two extreme views. They say that man can do action, but the deeds done, and the power of doing it, are both created by God. But this is quite meaningless. For if the deed and the power of doing it be both created by God, then man is necessarily compelled to do the act. This is one of the reasons of the difference of opinion about this problem.

As we have said there is another cause of difference of opinion about this problem, than the traditional one. This consists of the contradictory arguments advanced. For if we say that man is the creator of his own deeds, it would be necessary to admit that there are things which are not done according to the will of God, or His authority. So there would be another creator besides God, while the Muslims are agreed that there is no creator but He. If, on the other hand, we were to suppose that man cannot act freely, we admit thus he is compelled to do certain acts, for there is no mean between compulsion and freedom. Again, if man is compelled to do certain deeds, then on him has been imposed a task which he cannot bear; and when he is made to bear a burden, there is no difference between his work and the work of inorganic matter. For inorganic matter has no power, neither has the man the power for that which he cannot bear. Hence all people have made capability one of the conditions for the imposition of a task, such as wisdom. We find Abul Maali, saying in his Nizamiyyah, that man is free in his own deeds and has the capability of doing them. He has established it upon the impossibility of imposing a task which one cannot bear, in order to avoid the principle formerly disproved by the Mutazilites, on account of its being unfit by reason. The succeeding Asharites have opposed them. Moreover, if man had no power in doing a deed, then it will be only by chance that he may escape from evil, and that is meaningless. Such also would be the case with acquiring goodness. In this way all those arts which lead to happiness, as agriculture, etc., would become useless. So also would become useless all those arts the purpose of which is protection from, and repulsion of danger, as the sciences of war, navigation, medicine, etc. Such a condition is quite contrary to all that is intelligible to man.

Now it may be asked that if the case is so, how is this contradiction which is to be found both in hadith and reason to be reconciled we would say, that apparently the purpose of religion in this problem is not to divide it into two separate beliefs, but to reconcile them by means of a middle course, which is the right method. It is evident that God has created in us power by which we can perform deeds which are contradictory in their nature. But as this cannot be complete except by the cause which God has furnished for us, from outside, and the removal of difficulties from them, the deeds done are only completed by the conjunction of both these things at the same time. This being so, the deeds attributed to use are done by our intention, and by the fitness of the causes which are called the Predestination of God, which He has furnished for us from outside. They neither complete the works which we intend nor hinder them, but certainly become the cause of our intending them — one of the two things. For intention is produced in us by our imagination, or for the verification of a thing, which in itself is not in our power, but comes into being by causes outside us. For instance, if we see a good thing, we like it, without intention, and move towards acquiring it. So also, if we happen to come to a thing which it is better to shun, we leave it without intention. Hence our intentions are bound and attached to causes lying outside ourselves.

To this the following words of God refer: "Each of them have angels, mutually succeeding each other, before him and behind him; they watch him by the command of God" [Qur'an 13.12]. As these outside causes take this course according to a well-defined order and arrangement, and never go astray from the path which their Creator has appointed for them, and our own intentions can neither be compelled, nor ever found, on the whole, but by their fitness, so it is necessary that actions too should also be within well-defined limits, that is, they be found in a given period of time and in a given quantity. This is necessary because our deeds are only the effects of causes, lying outside us; and all the effects which result from limited and prearranged causes are themselves limited, and are found in a given quantity only. This relation does not exist only between our actions and outside causes, but also between them and the causes which God has created in our body, and the well-defined order existing between the inner and outer causes. This is what is meant by Fate and predestination, which is found mentioned in the Qur'an and is incumbent upon man. This is also the "Preserved Tablet" [Qur'an 85.22]. God's knowledge of these causes, and that which pertains to them, is the cause of their existence. So no one can have a full knowledge of these things except God, and hence He is the only Knower of secrets, which is quite true; as God has said, "Say, None either in heaven or earth, know that which is hidden besides God" [Qur'an 27.67].

A knowledge of causes is a knowledge of secret things, because the secret is a knowledge of the existence of a thing, before it comes into being, and as the arrangement and order of causes bring

a thing into existence or not at a certain time, there must be a knowledge of the existence or non-existence of a thing at a certain time. A knowledge of the causes as a whole is the knowledge of what things would be found or not found at a certain moment of time. Praised be He, Who has a complete knowledge of creation and all of its causes. This is what is meant by the "keys of the secret, " in the following words of God, "with Him are the keys of secret things; none know them besides Himself" [Qur'an 6.59].

All that we have said being true, it must have become evident how we can acquire our deeds, and how far they are governed by predestination and fate. This very reconciliation is the real purpose of religion by those verses and hadith which are apparently contradictory. When their universal nature be limited in this manner, those contradictions should vanish by themselves, and all the doubts which were raised before, about the contradictory nature of reason, would disappear. The existent things from our volition are completed by two things, our intention and the other causes. But when the deeds are referred to only by one of these agencies, doubts would rise. It may be said is a good answer, and here reason is in perfect agreement with religion, but it is based upon the principles that these are agreed that there are creative causes bringing into existence other things; while the Muslims are agreed that there is no Creator but God. We would say that whatever they have agreed upon is quite right, but the objection can be answered in two ways. One of them is that this objection itself can be understood in two ways; one of them being that there is no Creator but God, and all those causes which He has created, cannot be called creators, except speaking figuratively.

Their existence also depends upon Him. He alone has made them to be causes, nay, He only preserves their existence as creative agents, and protects their effects after their actions. He, again, produces their essences at the moment when causes come together. He alone preserves them as a whole. Had there been no divine protection they could not have existed for the least moment of time. Abu Hamid (Al-Ghazzali) has said that a man who makes any of the causes to be co-existent with God is like a man who makes the pen share the work of a scribe in writing; that is, he says that the pen is a scribe and the man is a scribe too. He means that "writing " is a word which may be applied to both, but in reality they have no resemblance in anything but word, for otherwise there is no difference between them. Such is also the case with the word Creator, when applied to God and the Causes. We say that in this illustration there are doubts. It should have been clearly shown, whether the scribe was the Creator of the essence (Jawhar) of pen, a preserver of it, as long as it remains a pen, and again a preserver of the writing after it is written, a Creator of it after it has come in touch with the pen, as we have just explained that God is the Creator of the essences (Jawahir) of everything which comes into contact with its causes, which are so called only by the usage. This is the reason why there is no creator but God — a reason which agrees with our feelings, reason and religion. Our feelings and reason see that there are things which produce others.

The order found in the universe is of two kinds: that which God has put in the nature and disposition of things; and that which surround the universe from outside. This is quite clear in the movement of the heavenly bodies. For it is evident that the sun and the moon, the day and night, and all other stars are obedient to us; and it is on this arrangement and order which God has put in their movements that our existence and that of all other things depends. So even if we imagine the least possible confusion in them, with them in any other position, size and rapidity of movement which God has made for them, all the existent things upon the earth would be destroyed. This is so because of the nature in which God has made them and the nature of the things which are effected by them. This is very clear in the effects of the sun and the moon upon things of this world; such also being the case with the rains, winds, seas and other tangible things. But the greater effect is produced upon plants, and upon a greater number, or all, on the animals. Moreover, it is apparent that had there not been those faculties which God has put in our bodies, as regulating them that could not exist even for a single moment after birth. But, we say, had there not been the faculties found in all the bodies of the animals, and plants and those found in the world by the movement of the heavenly bodies, then they would not have existed at all, not even for a twinkling of the eye.

So praised be the "Sagacious, the Knowing" [Qur'an 67.14]. God has called our attention to this fact in His book, "And He has subjected the night and the day to your service; and the sun and the moon and the stars, which are compelled to serve by His Command" [Qur'an 77.14]; again, "Say, what think you, if God should cover you with perpetual night, until the day of Resurrection" [Qur'an 16.12]; and again, "Of His mercy, He has made you night and the day, that you may rest in the one, and may seek to obtain provision for yourselves of His abundance, by your industry; in the other" [Qur'an 28.71]; and, "And He obliges whatever is in heaven or on earth to serve you" [Qur'an 18.73]. Further He says, "He likewise compels the sun and the moon, which diligently perform their courses, to serve you; and have subjected the day and night to your service" [Qur'an 45.12]. There may be quoted many other verses on the subject. Had there been any wisdom in their existence by which God has favored us, and there would not have been those blessings for which we are to be grateful to Him.

The second answer to the objection is that we say that the things produced out of it are of two kinds: essences and substances; and movements, hardness, coldness and all other accidents. The essences and substances are not created by any but God. Their causes effect the accidents of those essences, and not the essences themselves. For instance, man and woman are only the agents, while God is the real creator of the child, and the life in it. Such is also the case with agriculture. The earth is prepared and made ready for it, and the seed scattered in it. But it is God who produces the ear of the grain. So there is no creator but God, while created things are but essences. To this refer the words of God. "O men, a parable is propounded unto you, therefore, hearken unto it. Verily the idols which you invoke, besides God, can never create a single fly, although they may all assemble for the purpose; and if the fly snatch anything from them they cannot turn the same from it. Weak is the petitioner and the petitioned" [Qur'an 22.72]. This is where the unbeliever wanted to mislead Abraham, when he said, "I give life and kill" [Qur'an 22.260]. When Abraham saw that he could understand it, he at once turned to the conclusive argument and said, "Verily, God brings the sun from the east; do you bring it from the west."

On the whole, if the matter about the creator and the doer be understood on this wise, there would be no contradiction, either in Hadith or in reason. So we say that the word "Creator" does not apply to the created things by any near or far-fetched metaphor, for the meaning of the creator is the inventor of the essences. So God has said, "God created you, and that which you know" [Qur'an 2.260]. It should be known that one who denies the effect of the causes on the results of them, also denies philosophy and all the sciences. For science is the knowledge of the things by their causes, and philosophy is the knowledge of hidden causes. To deny the causes altogether is a thing which is unintelligible to human reason. It is to deny the Creator, not seen by us. For the unseen in this matter must always be understood by a reference to the seen.

So those men can have no knowledge of God, when they admit that for every action there is an actor. It being so, the agreement of the Muslims on the fact that there is no Creator but God cannot be perfect, if we understand by it the denial of the existence of an agent in the visible world. For from the existence of the agent in it, we have brought an argument for the Creator in the invisible world. But when we have once admitted the existence of the Creator in the invisible world, it becomes clear that there is no Creative agent except one by His command and will. It is also evident that we can perform our own deeds, and that one who takes up only one side of the question is wrong, as is the case with the Mutazilites and the Jabarites. Those who adopt the middle course, like the Asharites, for discovering the truth cannot find it. For they make no difference for a man between the trembling and the movement of his hand by intention. There is no meaning in their admitting that both the movements are not by ourselves. Because if they are not by ourselves we have no power to check them, so we are compelled to do them. Hence there is no difference between trembling of hand and voluntary movement, which they could call acquired. So their is no difference between them, except in their names, which never effect the things themselves. This is all clear by itself.

Divine Justice and Injustice

The Asharites have expressed a very peculiar opinion, both with regard to reason and religion; about this problem they have explained it in a way in which religion has not, but have adopted quite an opposite method. They say that in this problem the case of the invisible world is quite opposed to the visible. They think that God is just or unjust within the limits of religious actions. So when a man's action is just with regard to religion, he also is just; and whatever religion calls it to be unjust, He is unjust. They say that whatever has not been imposed as a divinely ordained duty upon men, does not come within the four walls of religion. He is neither just or unjust, but all His actions about such things are just. They have laid down that there is nothing in itself which may be called just or unjust. But to say that there is nothing which may in itself be called good or bad is simply intolerable. Justice is known as good, and injustice as bad. So according to them, polytheism is in itself neither injustice nor evil, but with regard to religion, and had religion ordained it, it would have been just and true. Such also would have been the case with any kind of sin. But all this is quite contrary to our hadith and reason.

As to hadith God has described himself as just, and denied injustice to himself. He says "God has borne witness that there is no God but He; and the angels and those who are endowed with wisdom profess the same, who execute righteousness" [Qur'an 3.16]; and "Your God is not unjust towards His servants;" and again, "Verily, God will not deal unjustly with men in any respect; but men deal unjustly with their own souls" [Qur'an 41.46]. It may be asked, What is your opinion about misleading the people, whether it is just or unjust, for God has mentioned in many a verse of the Qur'an, "That He leads as well as misleads the people?" [Qur'an 10.45]. He says, "God causes to err whom He pleases, and directs whom He pleases" [Qur'an 14.4]; and, "If we had pleased, we had certainly given every soul its direction" [Qur'an 32.11]. We would say that these verses cannot be taken esoterically, for there are many verses which apparently contradict them — the verses in which God denies injustice to himself.

For instance, He says, "He likes not ingratitude (Kufr) in His servant" [Qur'an 39.9]. So it is clear that as He does not like ingratitude even from them, He certainly cannot cause them to err. As to the statement of the Asharites that God sometimes does things which He does not like, and orders others which He does not want, God forbid us from holding such a view about him, for it is pure infidelity. That God has not misled the people and has not caused them to err will be clear to you from the following verses: "Wherefore be you orthodox and set your face towards true religion, the institution of God, to which He has created man kindly disposed" [Qur'an 30.29]; and, "when your Lord drew forth their posterity from the lions of the sons of Adam" [Qur'an 7.171]. A hadith of the Prophet says "Every child is born according to the divine constitution."

These being contradictions in this problem we should try to reconcile them so that they may agree with reason. The verse, "Verily, God will cause to err whom He pleases, and will direct whom He pleases" [Qur'an 14.4] refers to the prearranged divine will, with which all things have been endowed. They have been created erring, that is, prepared to go astray by their very nature, and led to it by inner and outer causes. The meaning of the verse, "If We had pleased, We have given unto every soul its direction" [Qur'an 35.9], is that He thought of not creating people ready to err, by their nature, or by the outer causes, or by both, though He could have done so. But as the dispositions of men are different the words may mislead the one and direct the other. For these are the verses which speak of misleading the people. For instance, "He will thereby mislead many, and will direct many thereby: but He will not mislead any thereby except the transgressors" [Qur'an 2.24]; and, "We have appointed the vision which We showed you" [Qur'an 17.62], and also the tree cursed in the Qur'an, and the verses about the number of angels of hell. "Thus does God cause to err whom He pleases and He directs whom He pleases" [Qur'an 74.34]. It means that for evil natures, these verses are misleading, as for the sick bodies even good drugs are injurious.

The Day of Judgment

Come the Day of Judgment, some believe that the body will be different from our present body. This is only transient, that will be eternal. For this also there are religious arguments. It seems that even Abdullah ben-Abbas held this view. For it is related of him that he said, "There is nought in this world of the hereafter, but names." It seems that this view is better suited to the learned men because its possibility is based upon principles, in which there is no disagreement according to all men: the one being that the soul is immortal, and the second is that the return of the souls into other bodies does not look so impossible as the return of the bodies themselves. It is so because the material of the bodies here is found following and passing from one body to another, i.e., one and the same matter is found in many people and in many different times. The example of bodies cannot be found, for their matter is the same. For instance a man dies and his body becomes dissolved into earth. The earth ultimately becomes dissolved into vegetable, which is eaten by quite a different man from whom another man comes into being. If we suppose them to be different bodies, then our aforesaid view cannot be true.

The truth about this question is this question is that man should follow that which he himself has thought out but anyhow it should not be the view which may deny the fundamental principle altogether. For this would be denying its existence. Such a belief leads to infidelity, on account of a distinct knowledge of this condition being given to man, both by religion and by human reason, which is all based upon the eternal nature of the soul. If it be said whether there is any argument or information in the Law about this eternal nature of the soul, we would say that it is found in the Qur'an itself, where God says, "God takes unto himself the souls of men at the time of their death; and those which die not He also takes in their sleep" [Qur'an 39.43]. In this verse sleep and death have been placed upon the same level, on account of the change in its instrument, and in sleep on account of a change in itself. For had it not been so it would not have come to its former condition after awakening. By this means we know that this cession does not effect its essence, but was only attached to it on account of change in its instrument. So it does not follow that with a cessation of the work of the instrument, the soul also ceases to exist. Death is only a cessation of work, so it is clear that its condition should be like that of sleep. As someone has said that if an old man were to get the eyes of the young, he would begin to see like him.

This is all that we thought of in an exposition of the beliefs of our religion, Islam. What remains for us is to look into things of religion in which interpretation is allowed and not allowed. And if allowed, then who are the people to take advantage of it? With this thing we would finish our discourse.

The things found in the Law can be divided into five kinds. But in the first place there are only two kinds of things: indivisible and the divisible. The second one is divided into four kinds. The first kind which is mentioned in the Qur'an, is quite clear in its meanings. The second is that in which the thing mentioned is not the thing meant but is only an example of it. This is again divided into four kinds. First, the meanings which it mentions are only illustrations such that they can only be known by the far-fetched and compound analogies, which cannot be understood, but after a long time and much labor. None can accept them but perfect and excellent natures; and it cannot be known that the illustration given is not the real thing; except by this far-fetched way. The second is just the opposite of the former: they can be understood easily, and it can be known that the example is just what is meant here. Thirdly, it can be easily known that it is merely an illustration, but what it is the example of is difficult to comprehend. The fourth kind is quite opposite to the former. The thing of which it is an example, is easily understood; while it is difficult to know that it is an example at all.

The interpretation of the first kind is wrong without doubt. The kind in which both the things are far-fetched: its interpretation particularly lies with those who are well-grounded in knowledge; and an exposition of it is not fit for any but the learned. The interpretation of its opposite — that which can be understood on both the sides — is just what is wanted, and an exposition of it is necessary. The case of the third kind is like the case of the above. For in it illustration has not been mentioned because of the difficulty for the common people to understand it: it only incites the people to action. Such is the case with the hadith of the prophet, "The black stone is God's action on Earth," etc., etc. That which can be easily known that is an example, but difficult to know of which it is an example, should not be interpreted but for the sake of particular persons and learned men. Those who understand that it is only an illustration, but are not learned enough to know the thing which it illustrates, should be told either that it is allegorical and can be understood by the well-established learned men; or the illustration should be changed in a way which might be near to their understanding. This would be the best plan to dispel doubts from their minds.

The law about this should be that which has been laid down by Abu Hamid (Al Ghazzali) in his book, Al Tafriga bainal Islam wal Zindiga. It should be understood that one thing has five existences which he calls by the name of essential (Zati); sensual (Hissi); rational (Agli); imaginative (Khayali); and doubtful (Shilbhi). So at the time of doubt it should be considered which of these five kinds would better satisfy the man who has doubts. If it be that which he has called essential than an illustration would best satisfy their minds. In it is also included the following hadith of the Prophet, "Whatever the earlier prophets saw I have seen it from my place here, even heaven and hell;" "Between my cistern of water and the pulpit there is a garden of paradise;" and "The earth will eat up the whole of a man except the extremity of the tail." All these, it can easily be known are but illustrations, but what is the thing which they illustrate it is difficult to comprehend. So it is necessary in this case to give an instance to the people which they may easily understand. This kind of illustration, when used on such an occasion, is allowable; but when used irrelevantly it is wrong. Abu Hamid has not decided about the occasion when both the sides of the question — the illustration and the illustrated — be both far-fetched and difficult to understand. In this case there would apparently be a doubt, but a doubt without any foundation. What should be done is to prove that the doubt has no basis, but no interpretation should be made, as we have shown in many places in our present book against the Mutakallimun, Asharites and the Mutazilites.

The fourth kind of occasion is quite opposite to the former. In this it is very difficult to understand that it is an example, but when once understood, you can easily comprehend the thing illustrated. In the interpretation of this also, there is a consideration: about those people who know that if it is an example, it illustrates such and such a thing; but they doubt whether it is an illustration at all. If they are not learned people, the best thing to do with them is not to make any interpretation, but only to prove the fallacy of the views which they hold about its being an illustration at all. It is also possible that an interpretation may make them still distant from the truths on account of the nature of the illustration and the illustrated. For these two kinds of occasions, if an interpretation is given, they give rise to strange beliefs, far from the law which when disclosed are denied by the common people. Such has been the case with the Sufis, and those learned men who have followed them. When this work of interpretation was done by people who could not distinguish between these occasions, and made no distinction between the people for whom the interpretation is to be made, there arose differences of opinion, at last forming into sects, which ended in accusing one another with unbelief. All this is pure ignorance of the purpose of the Law.

From what we have already said the amount of mischief done by interpretation must have become clear to you. We always try to acquire our purpose by knowing what should be interpreted, and what not; and when interpreted, how it should be done; and whether all the difficult portions of the Law and Hadith are to be explained or not. These are all included in the four kinds which have already been enumerated.

CPSIA information can be obtained
at www.ICGtesting.com
Printed in the USA
BVOW08s2000171217
503018BV00001B/90/P